The Atlantic House
Regan Good
ISBN 978-1-934639-08-5

First Edition, First Printing 2011
Printed in the USA

Published by Harry Tankoos Books

Distributed to the trade by
Small Press Distribution
1341 Seventh Street
Berkeley, CA 94710
www.spdbooks.org

Cataloging-in-publication data is available from the Library of Congress.

Cover illustration: Jenny Hampe Endresen

THE ATLANTIC HOUSE

Regan Good

Harry Tankoos Books

2011

Table of Contents

I wished to see that seashore where man's works are wrecks; to put up at the true Atlantic House, where the ocean is land-lord as well as sea-lord, and comes ashore without a wharf for the landing; where the crumbling land is the only invalid, or at best is but dry land, and that is all you can say of it.

—Henry David Thoreau

This book is dedicated to Ruth Thompson Good.

The Marble Head

Do not trespass into the marble head.
White face latched in its ivy, demure in the shade.
Hours of blind sight sunk in the arbor.

You know the windows we say are its eyes.
(To say it officiates is to lie; to say
it presides endows it with an animal's right.)

Riotous in daylight; suspicious at night.
(To say it is conscious imagines it upright.
To say it is merciless implies it divine!)

Now it watches us wrongly. Hoarding the time.
Crazy with hunger. Demented with wine.
All the Concords in hoarfrost hang shriveled to chimes.

The Mirror

What was dug up should have stayed below.

—An iron bell, whose tone was shrill when I rang the clapper free.

—A mirror so black it can't reflect faces. A mirror
so useless to the present scene and derelict of function,
no thing was recorded but what was deep and low.

Heavenward the mirror lay.

The integrity of the ground was mirrored in its metals.

It must have frozen, thawed, and froze its face dead.

I thought: Here is the surface on which to see Nature,

but as I turned it to regard me, my face was *nil, nihil.*

The Marble Head at the Mouth of the Arbor

Black grapes fructify and split their skins.

(Behind the head, twigs snap like abacus beads.)

His is the mind we make out of nothing.

This is what listens. Not the marble thrones,
or the placid faces of the men in robes.
This is what listens, deep inside the head of the Greek.

And the love named Hagia Sophia?

She is a gaudy cake of butterfly marble and candelabras,
with a river of vinegar running straight through her heart.

Was it yesterday I said the sun was sickening?
Shimmering over the canker—

Shall we swear all the pears are golden on the tree?

And read the Holy Sonnets religiously?

Shall we plant the rose in remembrance in the garden thriving like paradiso?

O, but then the one like the inferno with its song—

The sun is hot on our backs—briefly.

Then the flower heads suffer.

Docked in the Sun

Who are you, freak with no tethers?
                                                  The sun cathedrals.

Walking toward metal wings, wooden hulls, wire nests, and cages.

A pylon swings from a ten-story crane
                                                  over the boatmen's heads.

Panes of glass in the fish house rattle in their sashes.

No birdcries. No seabirds blunt the air.

You there, walking through the air as if it were a tunnel.

There is no knowledge there, which is knowledge.

(A thousand gulls hang motionless in flight.)

Yet, nothing still. Rocks and roses. Rocks and boats.

Beached boats looking wicked and humped.

Boats made stranger by the sand.

Evergreens blasted to shadow and anchor.

(Wind whistles through this Styrofoam coffee cup.)

Five thousand voyages stunted in their course.

You there, dash down the dock, the planks—

Past pilings, metal bollards, thickly painted chains—

Still, I do not know what it is you seek.

The Willow Is a Place from which to Speak

Inside the yellow wickets, rain fell.

With numerous fluted blossoms, the whips hung down.

(Stunted yellow-trumpets and gray pussy-willow buds.)

Supple, stinging whips when taken by the wind.

The canopy was a wonder and swayed,
and individual whips twisted—
though most wept straight down to make the tree a cage.

Weeping willow, swaying cage.
Yellow lantern made of pale whips.
More like knotted ropes than boughs.

Inside the willow, the black twigs were heavy-soaked,
and rain and some thousand ticking,
browning parts fell past me to the ground.

In frost, in the vines of incremental yellows,
dried-out wickets, soft-rot niceties—

From here now, I thought, compose a place from which to speak

as the willow's whips swept downward
and sometimes twisted (very beautifully) at my feet.

Ridership

The horses were marvels,
Egyptian laborers hauling stones.
(Their velvet nostrils held droplets.)

In the black leaves the horses tossed their heads.

Dark with water, their hooves—blunt wax, tallow, horn, and nail—peeled.

Their furred fetlocks spiked and stiff with mud.

They balked and jangled at their bits.
They puffed and bloated their barrels.

Then they took the hill with thrashing heads to strike
a tableau against the Cheyenne lightning show.

On the hill the horses were as other as ever.

Moving in the magnificence of flank and haunch—

How light I was on their backs!
How agile in my seat, moving the metal rod between their teeth!

Up there Eye of all dust.
Up there Eye of all the varied grasses.

Now how solemn they swing their heads and how low.

I Went to the Ocean to Redeem My Gifts

Wavelets rushed the sands.

                    (Out there, the depths squalled & churned
                    from the center of their fathoms.)

Pebbles poured in tumults over rocks with pipes of iron ore.

Tide pools pooled in the black rock's hollows.

I looked for a portal in the Atlantic House.

Wavelets stroked and crashed, stroked and crashed,
                    sucking pebbles back and forth.

Dune grasses scored perfect circles in the dunes.

(With arms outstretched, blinded by loose, scintillating sands—)

When I looked up from Mansion Beach I saw
the mansion of its name—saw straight through
two windows left unblocked, two windows
flushing cold sunlight straight through a ruined room.

I was quiet and waited.
Waited until the light indicated: too late.

(I waited until there was no sound but the loads churning in their troughs.)

I built a fire on Mansion Beach—fed it newsprint,
lists, and drafts—a month's worth of words of little consequence.
Then watched the fire burning on the sand
named for the house still standing in my mind.

The Wind Came Pushing with It Sands

Centrifugal treetops bristled in the blue.

Shock of red leaf: unpocked, uncrimped.

I wandered deeper but was blinded by the leaf.

No red as bright unless blood let onto snow.

No celebratory exegesis of which the leaf is a symbol.

Take this hollow and make a spot of me, I
thought, until the water took my eye
                    and led me to its cape—

There I found a burst balloon tied to a tangled string.

It being a remnant, a shred of its former airy Self,
it made the beach vaster in its vista and colder in its view.

It once had been a bladder on the wind.

Once possessed a purple rage and hue.

Sailed headlong, I thought, like Christ,
the Laughing One, buoyant in His cosmologies.
Laughing at particulars and temporal things.

Now this rubber scrap, this broken wing.
(As a freckled crab dug itself in backwards at my feet.)

One Bee Escapes My Palm to Grub What Is Left of Air

Across the darkling yard, the black bell sounds.

The high note's tone is caught wide inside the open mouth
then darkens as it's swung around—
Like a baby laughing on a swing,
Silly, giddy, up!—then sickened, dizzy, down.

I have a bee inside my fist, hot and furious.

Its stinger is here, still thrumming in my fingers.

I'd waved a stick around my head then tried to crush it with a rock.
It sent its stinger in, sent its hook into my hand—

Now it grubs a circle in my palm.

I push it so it walks. I lift the needle off the skip.
I push it forward so its path is straight and living.

I think you are Queen and cannot be transformed.

Ten times I've pushed you, still you crawl to die.
The pity is in the grunt's desire and nothing promised otherwise.

Negative equation under the persistent sun:

One bee escapes my palm to grub what is left of air—

Iron Water

I carried the deceptive weight of shadows to the lake,
tried to ditch it in a pile of rocks.

                                        They held me slant.
I threw the gift—watery and dark.

Love, Truth, & Beauty Best, I thought I thought.

How simultaneously my eyes are sick and bright.

                                        The frost is in the field.

Dogs run with tags on, barking black tangles.

Sumac, willow. Buntings and swallows.

Milkweed broke open, releasing their stringy hearts.

No rations, no sirens. Impossible to walk straight
on the jagged rocks, the slippery humps of track.

A curve ahead. A curve behind.

The crows are kings of carrion; they scrape and caw.
Imperial in their hideousness, they break and cluster.

They break and settle their lustrous Selves two trees down the line.

Forever

Immense pines made a spade-shaped arch,
a buttressed canopy, a stately walk, a tunnel—

One side prairie, one side marsh.

Cattails unraveled their velveteen heads.

Crossed the rope bridge in slow motion.

A weak red sun rose and rain turned to snow.

A weak white sun. The weak white sun
shone weakly through the white sky.

No discursive praise. No immortality.

Bells rang as if from under water.

Evening was a black sail luffing darkly in irons.

(There are days when the whole choir sings—
at once, chords strike a glorious happiness,
reverberations like an aviary humming in my chest.)

The snow had stuck but then it turned to rain.

Common reeds stirred both above me and behind.

They rattled with frozen drops until their tussocks
made whipping, sodden sounds, and their
rod-straight culms clattered until they stopped.

To parse the wind is to ask nothing in return.

To the German Equestrian

A pheasant in the grass opens, suddenly, and the reflex is: shotgun.

The man with the bird pressed to his cheek was a Nazi,
but gentle with horses afterthefact.

The boy beating the barn rat to death
kept screaming: *Come on, die, you fucker.*

Trains come and go like the closing and opening of slaughterhouse doors.

A field becomes black with the overhaul.

In that field, the dog's mouth was hot with bird:
the bullet hole, a minor derailment in a mouthful of Godforsakenness.

The Rose Garden

Who can believe in the nothingness of her?
The peonies, white and magenta by the bed.
The cat smelled the sheets then slunk downstairs.

The birds outside say: *Look, there is room.*
Come out, come out.

They are a decadence. A Newfoundland.

Gorgeous black after the script of their shadowed messages.

Crying: *Look, we are meat-eaters. Come out.*

Mourning doves gray the air into corridors up into the eaves.

Remember what the morphine did.
Taking the mind past hearing
so the body had a sleeping head.

Imagine a bonfire of roses in that head?

A bonfire of roses from the fecund garden.
Rosettes barking to bright red like wolves.
And the ivory buds in the yard like molded wax.

Lord, do you love your servant?
Do you love your servant asking for Heaven?

The crows are the Heaven and the Hell.
The crows are the Beauty and the Bells.

In the garden the rosebuds open—
Acolytes of a thousand masterful nothings.

A White Stone in Water

Last night the world was changed by water.
(No one awake in the hornet-colored light.)

The wooden steps had just been painted and the dogs were running riot—

Crows poured languidly from their stations—
as the ivy-crazed house stood quiet.

I counted keys on the grand piano until the worst was over.

And when it was, I tossed my head and flung the windows open—

There was no blood; there was no fire.
Instead the dead became an object to be admired.
There was no ice; there was no fire.
There was a white stone sunk in a bowl of water.

Rhododendron and pachysandra jiggled with rain hours after it ended.

And the sun rose red as it will again and the dead ride on waxed and quiet.

(I mean the sun *sank* red and the flood-tide waters changed the world
as a hundred doors flew open—)

As I said, I tossed my head as in a parade for a grand occasion.

I flashed the world a happy face like a Mussorgsky brass come striding.

(I know I ate and drank that night, as the stone stood white in its water.)

That night passed slow and morning came crying
after the last hard breath of the dying.

And today the sun seems slow in rising
as my mind smokes and flares like a paper fire—

The Rubber Ball

I walked through the tunnel of trees.
Chinks in the new green cubed and swayed.

Chinks in the new green threw spots—
Or was it shadow?

There was hopscotch chalked to its winning cube.

An ice-cream truck cranked its plinking music.
(Berserk nursery rhyme on a maddening loop.)

I walked past honeysuckle smell.

Chinks of light cubed then stretched—
Chinks in the half-dark threw spots.

I nodded to the dark porches, the darker rooms.
Walked over stick-figure anatomies, criss-crossed tic-tac-toe.

Pigeons screwed airy stairwells into the navy blue.

I bounced my Blue American Ball to this:

I looked to find the keeper of the key.
And when I saw the road of darkest night,
I took the one that wound away from me.

I walked through the tunnel of the trees.
Giving back ideas of what was mine to keep.
And who had been the keeper of the keys.

I bounced my ball against the walk.
I threw it hard and caught it high.

The neighbor's cutlery clanked and rang.
Then the sky went dark and thunder came—

I walked past what had been the greater house,
whose steeple was now a needle in the rain.

Lights from the street lamps struck, then stayed, as
homing pigeons careened in tandem back into their cage.

A Stone Should Mark the Place

In a public park, fringed by wilderness.
No marker there, no sense of what occupied space—
the invisible drift that caused my state to break.

Two dogs, both wolves, rush and jangle as they race.

Dogs run with mouths open, growl in raucous, ferocious merriment.

Ancestral wolves push through the dogs' domestic faces.

Wet leaves, black waters, this strange and shifting place.

The natural law is wearing winter's face.

O, strange and shifting race, with mouths open, two dogs—

No, two *wolves* run toward me, and, still, nothing marks the place.

The Tall Grass Parts and Bends

A windlet moved through yellowed tips, then sank
to bend the dune grass back at the glossy juncture
of its nape, its bundled roots of shiny straw—

The thin wind

fanned forward first then beat the grass
into a pulsing rush of shining gloss,
polished by chaotic gusts of rapid light.

It beat the anchored tufts to golden rods and humps of living green.

The wind then reverted to a single string,
and moved upward to join the vaster wind of origin.

(I watch the movement dissipate in the final quiver of its wake.)

This monument to abstracted space has kept my mind awake for days.

(I'd forgotten there are planes and squares
and hoops and circles in the air—)

Though this was more a finger than a shape.

The sky is edged and inked beyond reckoning.

It holds a thousand papery secrets in its depths
and has blunted my approach. Retreat, retreat,
the darkness said, you are tethered to a jangling leash—

Hammer Pounding the Summer

Imagine it darkly. Imagine it illumined.
The birches' white lightning staggering the trees.
Queen Anne's lace with its birthmark, its anchor.

So hot today in the arbor—suddenly summer.
The amphitheater's frozen stage has melted.

No drama. No music.

Come be my scarlet master, hammer pounding the summer.

(Smacking the black flies and flicking them away.
Taming the hatchets wielded by hunger.)

Come hold my gaze, high up on the ladder, scarlet master.

Suddenly stricken, offing a stag, I pitch
one ravaged Medusa head below my feet.

Come be my master, here in the hot, fragrant arbor.

I, the wasted music of the flower, hovering above the stalk—

I think the fathers laid the woods calm
while they thrashed the arbor home to nectar—
smacking the black flies and flicking them away.

Come be my master, high up on this ladder.
(Me thinking: Be cruel now, be stringent.
Be the serpent beneath the flower.)

The grapes heavy, shrinking, hung—
wasted as they add their heads to my empire
with the flies in my eyes and my ears and my hair.

Hammer pounding the summer, be fruitful,
be merciless, as my hand blunders past the leaves—

Throw the bunches down into their steaming buckets!

Errant action of the hand—
You thrust yourself forward out of order.

Bishop Sleeves (For My Slim and Lovely Daughter)

1.

Unsolicited low light pools in the apple copse.

The fecal-flecked silkworm nests,
strung and hung nastily through warted sticks.

Dirty, webby hammocks woven around
pretty lemony petals so bitter to bite.

Light does not grow like money, or appreciate
by borrowing.

It spills from the orchard
—a liquid, mutable radiance—
Everywhere (imperfectly so)…

As in: The apple trees stand hung with fruit and filth.

2.

The heavy ship sinks.
Its anchor plumbs the plushy silt.
Rocks crush the fo'c'sle and the ship begins to melt.
Sodden structure, sunken ship rotting where it lay.

Unlike the future garden
where I will be vigilant,

                                        noting the composites
                                        of these varied inflorescences,
                                        arranged so cleverly:

umbel, raceme, catkin, and whorl.

(How unlike the mitten-like mass of the fetal limb bud.)

I so prefer the panicle to the spike, though clover
is a honeyed-head thing just as my baby's brain
is a pomegranate full of blood.

Her head here in my palm, heavy as an iron ball.
Burning, burning with energy and nascent thought.

(I did the hand-smocking on her bib and urged the wind
                                        into her bishop sleeves.)

Such an engorged and slippery fish she is,
                                        with such frantic flailing spindlings!

Child: I smell the cradle cap on your throbbing fontanel
and fear your future sufferings. And that of all animals.

A Child Named Murder

We'll name our firstborn Murder.

She'll grow into her name.
Innocence obliterated; experience is her world.

She'll protest, of course.
It is natural for a babe to wish the springtime
When the Kingdom's waste.

When we call her from her toys of nails,
Come, Murder, come and give your King a kiss.
Sickened, she'll see that we know best.

By constant definition, she'll be taught:
Goodnight, Murder. Be careful, Murder.
Murder, I know what you are. Murder,
My cuckoo, born under a defunct star.

Your power is in your havoc.
You are made of certainty.

No will can change a bad seed's course.
Maps will drive this child insane!

Nothing can be divided. She owns it all.
There'll be no peace, though she'll splutter
Out her virtue on top her rocking horse.

And though the gift that she's been given
Is called autonomy, she'll see it as her prison.

She'll dismiss the murky sacred
For the metal of the profane.

O, Murder, my little kingdom,
All this mayhem for a name!

First Middle Last

Then let them anatomize Regan,
see what breeds about her heart:
Is there any cause in nature,
that makes these hard hearts?

—King Lear

You lost a rat, lost a dog,
Then drove away your dove.

By hothead crown and vitriol
You divided I to three,
Though your kingdom broke in two.

All my names plotted to pervert.
Named Regan for the princess
And the traitor in us all.

Then Maud for further heartbreak.
Shrill I am for that, and cold.
(I drive my men to rant like fools.)

Then Good to balance out the bad.
(Though no amount of good
Could fix this crooked hand.)

As a child you'd mock me: "So young and so untender?"
I'd curtsy back, "So young, my lord, and true."
To think a pup of yours could prove unkind.
Collared nightly, yapping at the pole.
My shadowed self lost faith in its intentions.

You rail, "I gave you all!"
To that I'll counter: In good time you gave it.
Your All's a slosh of bitterness in my cup.
I'd give it back to walk in innocence again.

Cock-eyed, daisy-chained, maundering on the heath.
A mouse was hungry in your mind,
So you fed it phantom cheese.

Good was the very Nothing, Nothing gave.

All three so untender, so unkind?
I think not. I think not.

I'd curse myself, my fate, my mind,
But for what I know to be base substance.

Does no one know the good I am?

The King's reduced to mincemeat by his Jester.
O, Cordelia, Cordelia: I am your sister.

Was Not Trusted, Was Not Taught

It's a black-weather day with no sun and no change.

Sun flashes in the iron sky.
Sun shines in the iron sky like a timpano.

Rain pops off giant leaves turning our beds to mud.

Bitterest down there, but ceremonial.

(In the forsythia tunnel the yellows were trumpets!)

Our skin itched from bites, from thorns.
Whatever song was sung was buried in the dirt.
It hummed, it hummed and I rocked to its rhythm,
I beat the dirt like a drum. I took pity. I took it.

I made the children be quiet. I told them sharply, *Stop crying.*

Beware the blue jays with their pointed black peaks.

Breathe when they aren't looking. Suck your fists if you have to.

Pity protects you. (I jammed my fingers in their mouths.)

They were not trusted, were not taught
to put their heads into the fragrant air,
to bravely smell the white and magenta apple spheres
fanning from the gnarled sticks.

Better lie low in the mud with its warnings.

It's a black-weather day with no sun and no change.

Today I Will Take My Large Tin Funnel

And pour my father into the jar where my mother used to live.
There their flaked bones and ashed tissues
will mingle as they would have wanted it.

His ash has spilled onto the metal slats
from the ragged edge of the cardboard
box in which the man was mailed to me.

Now he dusts the prow of our earthly ship—
the searing slats of aluminum where the landlord's
pea tendrils spindle, grope, then crisp.

Birdsong screeches over my activity,
distracting me from the spire to my right,
now a needle in my eye, though it does not sting.
(I do not care to be solved that way, as if I ever did.)

My brother's ashes are like flakes of pharaoh's gold,
meaning he could be anywhere, tossed into the air
off a California cliff. He is in all the gold I wear—
and he shines on my wrists and at my neck tonight,
even as I write.

Ruth was scattered under the Japanese maple tree.
She salted our Connecticut corn with alien tears.
There she stays—dispersed in handfuls from this jar
by the man now poured from a patented plastic sleeve.

What ash of hers clung to the jar's rutted declivities
now resides with my father's in perpetuity—
Though in truth all three are nowhere now:
Sean Richard, my brother; Paul Joseph, my father.
And Ruth Thompson, my gentle Zen-nun mother.

The Carousel Horses

Funny clowns, lovely laughter!
The horses' white saddles! Their red-painted bridles!
Their gold-painted teeth!

Coming on them chained shut, shut down,
I slipped, then stamped, then slipped again—
I stamped and stamped the steel cold down.

Fingered a soft, blunt ticket in my pocket.

(Lights on in the workers' trailers.)
(Small fairground by the dirty river.)

The Ferris wheel's buckets swung in the frieze.
The highway whistled: wind through a pipe.

O, but up close. Funny clowns. Lovely laughter!
The horses' red bridles! Their gold-painted teeth!

Rounding the round of their mechanized round.
Latched to the circle of tent silks and cranks.
See the discord of their half-lurch up or down?
Each stuck where the music last struck its chord.

(Yet, they won't be still, these flattering tassels.
Will not be still, this whirling toy with its smiling gashes.)

The horses twirl: lit wicks on a champagne pond.
Feckless grunts that could pull the sun.
Nostrils busted breathless in laughter.
High-stepping hooves extended and raised!

(The tattered ribbons flick, they snap.)

The mechanic sets the Ferris wheel turning.
He tips the metal cages and wipes the benches down.

Behind him the carousel horses preen in their colors.
They prance their garish mime, their eager pomp.

(They won't be quiet, these sailing horses!
Will not be still, this candied joy with its ropy tassels!)

To look closer is to see the war.
To look closer is to see O, *I fight*
The war that is my sailing circle.
The war that is my twisted bit.

We lurch and buck toward our end.
We are wooden-headed in the sunlight.
Then warhorses in the evening:

a frosted constellation poised to ravage in equipoise.

We Wanted to Catch It in a Gold Goblet

We wanted to catch it in a gold goblet. Blue estuary—
blue long leaden arms of Stygian night
stretched across the frozen ground in full daylight.

We thrust our breastbones out to catch the flying hooks.

By then the meat was in our wings—hinged joints
allowed the wingtips to touch first in front, then directly
above our heads, and finally to meet (fully extended) at our backs.

These wings were white and tightly needled to my frame.
But they slowed me down, they slowed my run.
They slowed my rotten progress to its end.

My mind: a remnant still of that crisp shell of nothing.

Push this automatic hand now the drugs are gone.

Irises once jammed with vistas, platforms, approaches.

Now: Pluck the hard hair from its glycerin sleeve.

This arctic sunset the colors of a Portuguese Man o' War.

The Rose

I had a goal. It was like a rose—red and open to the sky.

Tagged with sparse leaves. Scarce blunted thorns.

It was so rich, this rose. So red. So high above
the gate, so glazed in salt, so thunderously deep.

All caverns and fleshy sweeps: a universe of fans.

The whorl of its configuration knit tightly to its vortex-nub.

The rose was wild but climbed straight up.

I was enchanted by its high-headed worthiness.
And the triumph of its stalk—

(No scratch or crimp or crisp ate at its velvet edge.)

It was like the plastic ones forged in verisimilitude.

Never. Even in ice-throes. Even when I saw my rose
frozen completely in its ever-openness did my strident striver
burst or leak. It held its shape, agape, a silted cup
engorged with snow. No bites; no bruising crease.

It was triumphal in its singleness.

And lauded its beauty above me in the street.

Yet it grew to be my witherment and drove me wild,
as it was perched so above my reach. I could
have cut it down, but in deference, I let it live—

The Scales

1.

Days and nights move past the house,
One room once streaked in inexorable red—

I walk past the Depression-era green houses.
God's body to you. Or good day. Or Mary's blood.

Some precious books and wooden figurines on a table.
In a bowl, ten dried figs: amber sacks filled with children's teeth.

Palsy to the middle kingdom this fine evening,
And to the gorgeous column of blackbirds flying.

Palsy to the restless night, the moon not descending.

The last dead leaves have not let go.
Blackbirds shudder high in the pine branches.

God's body to them.

Black ornaments like startled faces.
And my face, the same lovelorn, dying medallion.

Remember the small sleep, the rounded death.

2.

And so it comes again, the song and its justice.
The roses beating their faces against the wind.
The dead roses harboring their deep infections.

O, you think them God's body?
Because of the perpetual debit of mercy?

3.

The Hangman has eaten the figs and defecated us an orchard.
Whiskey bleeds my stomach as I walk the grounds.

Musics rise and fall in the blackbird's throat.
In my mind's historic snows, this is the first—as I

Come eating and drinking, tipping the silver scales of justice
Which have weighed an ounce of truth for a pound of lies.

I, in my red jacket, with snow falling, being bled slightly.

Wine, a bird full of blood, in my glass.

4.

Still, I cannot deny the palsy, or my breath
Parading like plumes of rifle smoke—

God's body to it, and Mary's blood.

And to the birds above: The ashes have nowhere to go.

You were born, you nothings, now lie down and stop protesting.

The Ladder

The wrought-iron bench spray-painted white
sits at the mouth of the arbor.

A ladder's strung up.

It teeters in the dark, knocking against the vines—

The clocks have swung past the appointed time.

Ladder of aluminum. Ladder of chalk. Ladder,

struck up through the branches dripping with freeze.
Struck up and abandoned in warmer weather
when the hive of hellions murmured protestations—

(The fruit hangs tough as raisins—it scours and scratches
the aluminum ladder inside the delinquent vines.
The ladder rocks and sways, and no one climbs.)

The house that owns this arbor is like a handless clock.
No one lives there though the shelves are stacked:
pots au chocolat, Limoges, gold-rimmed demitasses—

This house in like a handless clock, but the ladder is a point in time.

The October sun—a cast horse prostrate on its iron back.

One sunflower wrenched its seeded head to stare.
The Connecticut evening raw as if a wet sand milled the air.

Wasps ghost the windfall, each pithed and plundered
ravishment, each fallen, sundry fruit—

One has stung me fierce despite the cold.

Their hive is like a house of paper.
I'll put a candle to their order.

They will rise in hatred and indignation,
letting loose a thousand stings of retribution!

I'll watch their sparks extinguish as they fly.

The Pianist

Pigeons purr a summer furnace.
Not scared. Not scared.

Until a window's thrown open
And they fly—a gray glove, quickly
Stripped, flung wildly away—
My neighbor starts to play.

Practice, practice. He practices his scales.

Often he stumbles, he starts them again.

Always at noon, with the window wide open.
A white curtain blown out—

Hammers wholly wooden striking strings.

His fingers cartwheel up and down the keys.

Stairways and braids, stairways and braids.
Bass clef whirling its windmill Xs.
Left hand growling under the shining right.

Notes in order struck over and over—
Notes in the air making angles and corners.

A man in the woods walking in circles.
Without direction he says to himself:

This archway of trees is not Chartres Cathedral.
I must be the doorway. I am the steeple!
Abruptly he stops. The pigeons come back.
Then again with his preludes, etudes, and scales—

Black ivy tumbling in buckets of shade.
The pigeons, in circles, refusing to land.

The Imperfect

1.

If the imperfect is our Paradise,
                                        these are the bells of Heaven I hear.
The faint sound of small bells
                                        knocking against the neighbor's door.

2.

Today the rain was an estuary, gray as the Bastille in Paris's rainy season.

3.

This morning I counted the 88 keys on the grand piano,
                                    then played a scale nipping eight right-hand notes.

I played until the sun broke in, white with autumn.

4.

(Lucid go the days, though my stringent speech has left me hollow.)

5.

The neighbor's room has been washed and painted.
He saw past the metaphysics into the pulp that made the pages.

Pound out the Orient on my grand piano.

Creature without a castle, a black-and-white logic dooms us.

Eat from hand-painted Limoges, each plate painted for a season.

6.

Hand that hung out the string of bells,
                                                  you who cut yourself to pieces—
Here is a house where the attempt succeeded.

7.

If the imperfect is our Paradise,
                                                  those are the bells of Heaven I hear.

8.

I count the 88 keys on the grand piano.

My fingers nip the shining notes.

9.
                                                  Not a soul to talk to in this brilliant weather.

In the Garden on a Cold Night

1.

Scraps and tangles are the stars.
The air's turned every droplet into ice.

Down the path, two stone lions herald a formal entrance:

a winter garden wrapped in plastic sheets,
long flower beds of upturned earth
sprouting long oniony leaves (as Roethke writes).

                                        Up there

the children marched into the stinging air
off planks of springy evergreen.

                          Now these shriveled lilacs—
these crabbed, empurpled sickle-celled florets.

2.

Next door the neighbors mourn their moneyed patriarch.

(All day cars with headlights on arrived in full sunlight.)

The pale yellow house was lit from attic to earth.
Its evergreens were strung with giant outdoor Christmas lights.

The house appeared to be on fire or even the sun itself.

The field went black, square by square. From where I stood

one walked down the beaten path singing: *Perfect the imperfection*

of the setting sun, perfect to me because I imperfect come.

Whiskey Stole Sunday: Invisible Rider

The horses shifted on their horny feet.

Muck in the barn aisle; muck in the standing stalls.
Drunken bees grazed the rotting applemash,
as boney kittens leapt leukemic in the dust.

By the garden wrapped in black plastic sheets,
a flowering tree hung with wormy progeny.

Some fruits fell far and rotted where they lay.

In the stalls, the horses shifted where they stood.

I led one by a chain woven through two leather straps,
led him past fermented fruits to the center of the field.

There I braided his waxy tail to its ragged tip,
                                        then watched the segments slip apart.

(Only the straggled end retained its distorted knot.)

I dropped the chain and smacked his flank
                                        and watched his haunches pump away.

On the hill—martingaleless—the horse curvetted once.
Then stamped and snorted where he stood.

No chariot of mutable gas. Rider: You exist but do not live.

Your leathers hold the irons, ever leadenly directed
downward toward the silty pools from which the horses drink.

Earthly horses, these. They like the dirt. The cloudy silt.

The air smells hierarchic in their wake.

On the Porch One Night, I Thought I'd Listen

(No one was with me—I was alone.)
Someone had died and I hadn't stopped.
I was thinking and suffering hard that curse
I'd die from if persistent when words
and the world are inconsistent—where description
called for something where there was no thing.

Porch screens held back a depth of noise.

I was tired and useless to start the conversation.

(Crickets chirped a world of muted bells.)

The porch was just a thing of boards and nails.

(Just as I am memory and flesh.)

The trees were black, though some (it's true) were white.
(The birch trees grow crooked here, while
the black-trunked trees grow straight.)

The woods burned at my back with sugar, not with flame.

The fire at my feet shifted, spat, collapsed.

Embers squeaked when crushed by pinching tongs,

to fall like tiny silver bells or
                    tinkling chinks of Styrofoam.

Outside a steadiness persisted.

It was sound alone standing for the world.

My chair could rock and so I did—
                    but not for comfort or for sleep.

I rocked myself indivisible into the nightsounds of the keep.

These Winter Gardens

This weather is for greyhounds.

Inside the willow with its profusion of whips,
the wickets have made a lantern of light.

Winter crows you. You are glazed in ice.

The tight buds of beginning shine from their scales.

Dogs off their leashes, two greyhounds run circles,
taut on ballerina legs.

This garden is a machine of moving parts.

Pinwheel leaves, a white-stone path leads one deeper,
past the stone bird bath and its circle of dirty ice.

My categorical imperative is *Live free from fear*, yet still I am afraid.

The garden is deeper than we thought.

(A winter wracked with headaches and head colds.)

Read until the shining skull duly shines—

(I knew the whole of his moving parts intimately.)

Wrapped in plastic garbage bags: bulbs, perennials, flowering fruit trees—

(Once knew the machinations of his moveable parts by heart.)

One Winter Night at the Race Track

Gone the tonnage of horseflesh,
the hyper, sultry thoroughbreds—

Gone the horses breezing their barrels.

The race track was a white disc in snow,
a white-faced sundial over which shadows & hours
moved (as usual) all day and all night—

No winning, no losing, walking on top
crusted snow fully ten inches from the ground.

Then *whoosh* through a hole in the chainlink.

Hundreds of stalls with green-painted gates.

Tall trees cast black banners interspersed with rectangles of white.

Last time in such snow, the moon alone illuminated the track.

No horses then either, only horses as half-thoughts.

(Hear the hollow whistle of the locomotive wafting its sound away?)

Watch the shadows skitter and sway,
lunge with the gusts and do not be afraid.

Generic Birds & Specific

Up there, with last year's leaves,
high up where the tips terminate
and the branches push out their buds
(halved, quartered, clustered, peeled).

Where are the birds?

Whistling in the fronds.
Emanating from slits in the sky,
those airless feathered pockets
where they are sound alone.

Without the birds nothing but stuck
in this blustery room of my mind
where punishments are exacted,
freedoms denied.

How did this music get so mangled?
So tuneless?
Birds so small they squeak
at my will, at the lip of my face—

I see the others still hard at it,
routing the greased swoop
distant now like the Umbrian tower
where the abstraction took place
and I was as singular as
a single white pigeon feather
caught on a single raised nail.

Here they fly in the tall hedge,
with its scaffold of branches,
in and out, making entrances and exits,
until (with my two hands clapping) I
flush them into the surrounding air,
sending one straight up (into the sun itself,
it seemed) so that for one instant
each of its feathers was distinct.

No More These Unsightly Tricks

Pulled from the water, pulled from the sky.

Why does a thing not grow to its perfection?

Why doesn't each branch extend fully to its ruby tips?
Then explode in loveliness to fall complete and spent?

Each vacuole pumps fresh water for its eye.

What stunts and crimps and warps?
What blood nourishes these hatchlings?

Bloody thumbs stuffed with operatic joy.

(Up in the branches there were poetries
partly glimpsed.)

The burl of my heart is the fovea of their eyes.

So hot: iron rod through a hollow shoot.

Romantic hungry thresher: I need to go.

The sun said: Be alive in excellence
as you walk through this sun-drenched rain.

Be proud, proud horse, tripping through your glossy gaits.

What went ye out into the wilderness to see?

I know the ocean roars and turns inside a bell.
Return you to my sister Nature. In Her is where I dwell.

What I Saw and What It Said

(There—black shapes in the yellow leaves.)

I swear I waited to hear them with my eyes.

I saw a bird in a dog's mouth.

The dog shook its head until it seemed the bird there flew.

What could I know?

The bird had the placid look of a hanged man.

The dog held that languid animal in its mouth—
an animal that spoke by moving through the senses of other animals.

The dog could hear it.

The dog heard it through the blood collecting in its mouth.

You think I am wrong? That the dead bird speaks?

You know how it feels to hold something small
in your hands and want to crush it?

Now imagine it stays still and does not leave you.

The Owl and the Peacock

1.

Death snatched thrice. The garish roses lived.
Each with a spider at its heart. The owl
is a bird with an alpine head—an image
of wisdom and of the wandering dead.

2.

We turn to the peacock. See order in its fantail.
Worry its beauty into reason which without reason dies?
We know now they too are caught in hyperbole:
The empire of God. The laurel tree.

3.

The living owl's eyes cannot move, and so it turns
its entire head to the direction of its prey.

4.

The owl and peacock, what do they conspire to mean?
I say: My devotion to these birds has turned
my blood to lead, and the owl is a bird that lives,
and the one that meant death is dead.

The Train

(I recall its bright conception, how it felt to touch it,
let it go, & watch it spin—)
                                        I rode in a fever:

Bright bolt of cloth pulled through a metal ring.

Rode past a white farmhouse. Its black door gave it distinction.

                                        (No deception in winter.)

Rode past a black dog locked in a corncrib.

Snow piled in spiny ridges along branches of tree and bush.

(The toy spun on—it was a mechanized bird
                                        with turning wings, amply greased.)

Rode through a truss bridge high over a dry creek.
Rode past switch tracks and farmland in parcels.
Rode in the train car banded by sunlight.

Eventually we rode past a low wall of fire.

It burned in the ditch-like cradle of the berm.
It burned on my window's side for an hour.
I watched it through the window as long as I could stand.

The fire made a mansion of my senses (the toy spun on),
rooms on fire and windows breaking and curtains flapping.
So much like the spirit, but unlike this wet, black, restless thing.
Despair is a one-note song, and I plucked it up with crazed
happiness and counterpointed high vertiginous trills.

Then we crossed the river, spanning a mile across.

At the Mississippi's center, I felt a shifting in myself.
Something central unfolded symmetrically,
fixing the East behind, the West in front.
It centered the flowing river always in-between.

(The bird, stuck in a state of mechanical shuddering, came
unstuck and lurched to face the opposite direction.)

And I began to laugh and laugh a crazy laugh.

I laughed—a Cosmic Christ, laughing at the World.

I laughed like Him, recalling what had come before:
                                        the barking dog, the farmhouse door.

(The toy spun on, the gold bird preened and snapped its metal beak.)

I laughed and laughed a crazy laugh, withdrawing swiftly from the East.

As the bird sang songs in apogee, hopping circles on wire feet.

I Looked Beyond the Gates and Wished to Enter In

This cold spring. Snow in Apriltide.
Snow encasing buds in ice.

Small white rosebuds cut sharply by the Maker's knife.

Salt nourishes the climbing rose.
Consequently roses grow wildly by the sea.

Twice the gate was locked though I wished to enter in.

The tunnel was wet to wade and thousands of petals
fell all night past the goldfish frozen in the lily pond,
the gilded statues with their good-luck parts rubbed black.

Three times I threw my mind down the littered walk
as petals fell—dogwoods all from where I stood.

One mark for the Crown of Thorns, two
for each hand, and one for the long nail
driven deep into His overlapping feet.

No more the son of God than I, my face
raised to what was being driven down.
Three times I knocked but only once I entered in

to move through that slanted rain of white,
to taste the blood of my lord Jesus Christ.

The Atlantic House

1.

Load of rope, burnt rafter, scorched beam.

Beach grasses bend: orange, silver, hay-flake green.

Easy to weave into crosses or to braid.

The sea has shed some thousand ships out there, then carried
portions to the shore.

You can carry the load of rope if you can lift it.

Knotted rope encrusted with sand,
fleas, clear (nearly microscopic) shrimps.

Lighthouse without a keeper.

The sea's static rant compelleth. Allow me:

This rope, beached like a body, is yours if you can lift it.

2.

I too miss the advent of the strict command.
So, blessings to your foundered fleet, Captain.

The sea reflects the "mercy of his means."

And so I take for my conceit a ship,
slime-moldered, buoyed by an ocean's worth of green.

The ship struck out into the waves, and the sea frothed forth
the usual matters of the brain.

The moon sucked the pebbles back in tumult to the shore.

Cast out your anchor if you can.

Ship at sea, listing there above its hook.
Listing where the hook can't touch the floor.

A sunken ship—five thousand ships.

3.

                                        Rain on the roof,
onto the leaves, making them wave and dip
incessantly, all night, nodding, nodding the leaves—

Five thousand wrecks offshore.

Rain pops and streams and guzzles at the house
as if to scour some blood or blight.

From that house I saw two lives (neither exactly mine) go forth.

As the sea churned forward a thousand shovelsful of salt.

4.

By the kitchen window,
a cardinal appears—
shock like a bright blood droplet
on a white cloth. Terrible.
Sane.

5.

Pull into the fog.

Ropes, sails, the once buoyant hull where many men
now sleep badly in the belly of the lady ship.

Pull deeper in.

6.

Love, to be in this house is to be a ship in the wind—

the windows are portals cranked open to the elements
through which no wave shall pass.

                                                            But the wind comes in,
displacing things
(papers, writing instruments)
as the pine boughs bluster and heave (lunge wildly, in fact).

The rain miles from here so that sometimes I see great shafts of bullion.

Even now I would turn this ship backwards
into the sun—directly
(if you asked me to return), or I will remain in the wind
without a compass or a chart.
Hopeless to try (even with such a delicate instrument)
(hopeless, striving instrument)—
to direct what has no direction backwards,
to turn this "wooden world"
through the ancient timber that constitutes the sea—

7.

Fontanel, battered by wind, by rain.
Slanting rain mixed with ocean spray.

Life is a business, not good cheer.

(Broad bone like the battering prow of the lady ship.
I heaved forward into the ocean's crash—)

What loves us encourages us to rot.

Life is a business, not good cheer.
I say this to the gray waves, and the green.

A jutting, rotted maidenhead—my battered, thrusting diadem.

8.

Who calls? Who calls us shipwrecked?
Who calls and slams the stern into the wave?

Terror plus Beauty equals Sublimity.

The ship is lost, the ship is not wrecked.

All quiet in the hull. All quiet in the cargo space
where the waters darkly suck and run.

9.

Slatternly ship on an amorphous sea.

Cast out your anchor if you can.
Cast out your anchor, iron hook on iron bar.

The anchor pierced the surface with its spike.

Drifted down through this airless world.

A hook and string that could not reach.

Without anchorage in the open sea.

Go, go, ship.

Hotly slide across the glass salt cake.
You fly fast
across as Elsewhere is
splendidly arranged
on the other side.
Go.

All the sun's weight now dazzles in the brine.

10.

Go quickly: My love, my love, I am always here.
The Atlantic House is everywhere.

Notes

I Went to the Ocean to Redeem My Gifts: Takes place on Mansion Beach, Block Island, Rhode Island.

The Rose Garden: The first line is from Thomas Wolfe's *Look Homeward, Angel*: "We can believe in the nothingness of life, we can believe in the nothingness of death and of life after death—but who can believe in the nothingness of Ben…?" The mention of the "servant" directly borrows language from a poem by Jenny Mueller called "The Plaintiffs," specifically from her phrase "tortured servant."

A Stone Should Mark the Place: References "Anecdote of a Jar" by Wallace Stevens.

Bishop Sleeves (For My Slim and Lovely Daughter): The title in parentheses is the title of a poem by my mother, Ruth Good.

The Scales: Borrows an image from one of Lance Philips's poems, specifically the image of the roses beaten by the wind.

The Ladder: A cast horse is one that has flipped on its back and cannot right itself.

The Imperfect: Borrows a line from the poem "The Poems of Our Climate" by Wallace Stevens.

No More These Unsightly Tricks: This title is a line from *King Lear*, as is "Return me to your sister."

The Atlantic House: The book's epigraph and the poem's title is taken from *The Beach*, by Henry David Thoreau. The repeated line, "Life is a business, not good cheer," is taken from the seventeenth-century poet George Herbert's poem "The Temple."

Acknowledgements

Some of the poems in this book first appeared in the following journals:

American Letters & Commentary; *The Antioch Review*; *Asheville Poetry Review*; *The Cortland Review*; *Fence*; *Field*; *Hampden-Sydney Poetry Review*; *LIT*; *The Literary Review*; *New Letters*; *Northwest Review*; *The Paris Review*; *Pool*; and *The Winter Anthology*.

Several poems appeared in a limited edition chapbook called *The Imperfect*, published by Westown Press in 2005.